John Maynard Keynes

A short, precise, easy to understand and most of all **CORRECT** depiction of his theory.

Autor Andrés Ehmann

Keynes

A short, precise, easy to understand and most of all CORRECT depiction of his theory

I. Preface

This booklet or essay is a summary of the website www.economics-reloaded.com. This website is not yet finished, but it will be completed by July 2015. The German version, (www.economics-reloaded.de) and the Spanish version (www.economics-reloaded.es) are already accessible and more or less finished.

For the sake of clarity we have chosen to relinquish the use of direct quotes in this booklet (especially from Keynes' The General Theory of Employment, Interest and Money). If you are looking for a discussion of The General Theory of Employment, Interest and Money that draws directly on the original text, you will find it on the aforementioned websites.

We have also chosen to limit our illustrations of Keynesian theory using examples and focus more on the theory, as we present examples extensively on www.economics-reloaded.com. We assume that the reader is familiar with the contemporary crises and problems and is therefore able to see the relevance of the ideas presented in this booklet.

Keynes is by far the most-quoted economist of all times. Almost no day passes without a newspaper or a television talk show referring to his theories. If there is a debate on economic issues on an internet forum, it is almost certain that someone sooner or later will make an argument that implicitly or explicitly draws on Keynesian theory.

Nevertheless, very few people have read The General Theory of Employment, Interest and Money, even among economists in academia.

In public and academic debate, Keynes's thinking is commonly reduced to certain simple statements that are neither representative of Keynesian theory nor well-suited to illustrating the fundamental differences between classical/neoclassical theory and Keynesianism. In such debates Keynes is reduced to expansive fiscal policy, namely that in case of recession the government should expand demand and, in case of boom, should reduce it. In other words, government should make use of an anticyclical policy.

If these were the basic claims made by Keynes it would be easy to refute his theory. But whoever claims that the current crisis in Greece is the result of a Keynesian expansive fiscal policy and that this demonstrates that Keynesian theory is flawed, does not understand Keynesian theory or what is occurring in Greece. This essay is written in 2015 and Europe is still struggling with the consequences of the financial crash of 2008.

Mainstream economists who cling to neoclassical concepts and take Greece as confirmation of their way of thinking can be assured that the most prominent and important economist of the 20th century was well aware that an increase in public spending only leads to a flash in the pan if the demand induced by an increase in public spending is fully satisfied by goods from foreign countries. If the Greek government increases public spending by increasing the number of public employees and they buy, for instance, German cars, they stimulate the German economy, but the indebtedness of Greece will increase. Keynes should not be underestimated.

The fact that only a few arbitrarily canonised concepts have survived from what is otherwise a complex set of theories is not only true of Keynesian theory; it is also true of the ideas of Adam Smith, David Ricardo, Jean Baptiste Say, Vilfredo Paret, and others. On www.economics-reloaded.com we show the difference between the public's perception of these authors and their original texts. Moreover, on www.economics-reloaded.com and its sister pages we demonstrate how this eclectic and arbitrary selection of concepts may be explained. For this reason we will not repeat these topics here.

The reduction of some authors' work to certain simple concepts is not as dramatic as it is in the case of Keynesian theory because macroeconomic problems cannot be discussed without a clear understanding

of the terms used, and Keynesian theory meticulously specifies its terms. If we talk about savings, money, capital or interest rates, we must first have a clear understanding of their definition. By using these terms without a clear idea of what they mean, as often happens in classical/neoclassical theory or in public debate, the terms become associated with functions that they do not have and meaningful debate becomes impossible.

Keynesian theory is not the answer to all economic questions and it never was intended as such. However, Keynesian theory is the foundation upon which all discussion about economic problems must be based.

What is this booklet about? It seeks to provide an easy-to-understand, clear, precise and, most of all, accurate presentation of Keynesian theory. It also hopes to be accessible even to those who have never held a book on macroeconomics in their hands, but who have wondered if the interest rate will remain stable if aggregate savings increases or if the central banks will print more money; or why we see bubbles only in certain sectors of the economy, such as stock markets, housing markets, gold, etc.; or what would happen if the banks were to pass on to their customers the advantageous refinancing possibilities offered by central banks.

We have endeavoured therefore to write a booklet that can be read without great effort in 20 hours and which organises the concepts and ideas in such a way that a meaningful discussion becomes possible. If people talk about capital, money, interest rates or savings it must be clear what they mean by these terms.

II. Classical Theory

II.1 What Keynes does not Question: the Efficiency of the Market

It is well known that Keynes did not distinguish between what are now referred to as the classical and neoclassical authors. In other words, he made no distinction between classical authors such as Adam Smith, David Ricardo, Jean Baptiste Say, John Stuart Mill and neoclassical authors such as Alfred Marshall, Vilfredo Pareto, Léon Walras, and Carl Menger. He referred to everything that had been written before him as "classical theory".

We will not address herein the problem with the terms classical and neoclassical theory, and we refer the reader to www.economics-reloaded.com for this discussion instead. In brief, however, if we explore those concepts not focused on by Keynes (those other than the concepts of money, savings, capital, and interest rates) there is little resemblance between the authors. If we examine the concepts of money, savings, capital and interest rates as addressed by Keynes, classical and neoclassical authors can be considered as one group. For the scope of Keynesian analysis this is correct, and Keynes correctly considered them all as belonging to the same group. If we consider those concepts not focused on by Keynes, there is little resemblance between these authors. For example, there is very little resemblance between Jean Baptiste Say and David Ricardo, two classical authors, and no resemblance between Alfred Marshall and Léon Walras, two neoclassical authors.

Classical economists or neoclassical theory actually do not exist. We address this issue in more detail on www.economics-reloaded.com. Classical economists and neoclassical theory are based on the same wrong assumptions regarding capital, money, savings and interest rates, and are therefore subsumed into one group (as Keynes did) and labeled as classical theory.

We have likewise chosen not to discuss in this booklet economic tendencies such as neoliberalism, the Austrian School, monetarism or ordoliberalism which, as with classical/neoclassical theory, are based on erroneous ideas about capital, savings, money and interest rates. However, we do discuss these in detail on www.economics-reloaded.com.

From here on we will only refer to economic thinking before Keynes as classical theory, as Keynes himself did. Incidentally, it is often remarked that neoclassical theory is characterised by something called a "marginal revolution". On www.economics-reloaded.com we demonstrate that such a thing never happened, because the concept of marginality was already present in the works of David Ricardo and Adam Smith. There are therefore additional reasons why the distinction between classical and neoclassical economics is of little use.

The basic thesis of classical economics is that personal interest (of individuals, companies and households) and general interest coincide. The most famous example of this is the one concerning the baker and the butcher found in Adam Smith's The Wealth of Nations. The baker does not produce bread to make us happy, but to earn money, and the only way he can earn money is to produce bread as well and as inexpensively as possible.

In the view of classical economics, competition is, therefore, a means of promoting general prosperity.

The well-known notion of homo oeconomicus, whose only aim is to maximise his own profit, can only be understood in this context. In other words, without competition, homo oeconomicus is not a useful construct. Competition and decentralised information processing through prices (see below) are the pillars of a market economy, they guarantee the optimal use of resources and are not criticised by Keynes.

On www.economics-reloaded.com we discuss many systems where system-driven control does not work, for instance in jurisprudence, in public education, or in public administration.

System-driven control means that no external control is needed to guarantee the optimal use of resources. A private company that does not make optimal use of its resources will disappear, because its competitors have an incentive to be better. Public administration is not exposed to competition and therefore has no incentive to improve performance.
If systemic control does not occur naturally, it must be introduced artificially through mechanisms that are as impactful as the control mechanisms of markets and competition.

A second crucial element in market economies that Keynes acknowledged is the decentralised processing of information through prices. Prices reflect the scarcities and the changes in economic structures, and individual market players know better how to react on these changes than a distant governmental central planning commission.
Prices are signals of scarcity, but they also lead to a reduction in scarcity because prices serve as an incentive to reduce the scarcity. High prices guarantee high profits.

These two concepts, competition and the decentralised processing of information through prices, help us distinguish between a market economy and a planned economy. In planned economies the coordination of economic activities is realised by a plan and a central planning institution. This requires that the central planning institution be as well informed as millions of individual market players, and this is never the case.

The individual entrepreneur is always better informed about his alternatives than a central planning institution, and a single household is always better informed about its needs and preferences than a central planning committee.

Decentralised planning through prices is, likewise, much more flexible than central planning by a governmental institution, and much faster when it comes to correcting erroneous decisions. A governmental institution is not only less well informed than a market player in a market economy, they also have less of an immediate incentive to correct bad decisions.

Competition and decentralised planning / information processing through prices are the two pillars of market economies and, though the opposite is often claimed, these fundamental principles are not questioned in Keynesian theory.

Lines of thought such as neoliberalism are not really new. Neoliberalism focuses on the importance of decentralised information processing through prices, leading to free cooperation between different market players. Driven by competition, this free cooperation will result in an optimal allocation of resources as compared with governmental intervention (which neoliberals claim distorts the allocation of resources). Neoliberalism can be summarised in one sentence: Everything that must be controlled can be controlled through the market mechanism and, whatever cannot be controlled should not be controlled. This version of a market economy goes a little bit too far, because if everything is decided by the market and what is not decided by the market should not be decided at all, there is no space left in the system for democratic decision-making.

Ordoliberalism claims that market economies tend to eliminate competition over the long run, a problem already mentioned in The Wealth of Nations. Companies will seek to avoid competition and will ultimately agree on prices at the expense of the consumer. Governmental intervention, for instance in the form of constraints on monopolies, trusts and pricing agreements, is necessary to guarantee sufficiently intense competition.

The problems of market economies, which are characterised by competition and by decentralised information processing, are well known. Market economies tend to bring about unequal distribution of the national product and, contrary to what classical theory teaches, do not bring about full employment, not even over the long term. Thus, there are two elements which are correct and not questioned by Keynes: competition and decentralised information processing. These lead to the optimal allocation of resources. Prices permit the allocation of resources in the best way possible because they reveal scarcities, and because competition obliges companies to allocate their resources in the most efficient way. In a market economy companies can and must work efficiently.

In classical economic theory, distribution of the national product is the result of remuneration for three different productive factors: labour, capital and land. The scarcer a productive factor is in relation to demand, the better it is compensated.

It is well known that the remuneration of labour can become so low that the political system becomes unstable. However, the government cannot adjust this remuneration as this would eliminate all incentives to pursue higher qualifications and to adapt to changes in the structure of the economy.

One answer to the problem of unequal distribution is the so-called social market economy. A social market economy does not intervene in the allocation of productive resources and thus it does not impede market players from responding adequately to scarcity, as happens in a planned economy. However, a social market economy does intervene when it comes to the distribution of the national product. The national product resulting from the functions of the market is redistributed through the tax system and through social transfers.

A market economy has little to say about unemployment. Some classical authors tend to elaborate verbosely on unemployment. We can summarise their views by saying that, in their view, unemployment does not exist. As this problem does not exist in their view, there is no need to resolve it either.

This is a crucial difference between Keynesian and classical theory, and all the lines of thought and schools which are based on the latter's concepts.

For the classical theorists, unemployment will disappear in the long run if workers relinquish excessive wage demands. For Keynes, unemployment is possible and cannot be eliminated by lowering wages.

II.2 Money or Capital: What does Savings Mean?

In order to speak about Keynes we must first sort through the terms we use. On www.ecomomics-reloaded.com we show that both Adam Smith and David Ricardo used the term "capital" and "money" as synonyms, sometimes even in the same paragraph.

This had fatal consequences. Karl Marx disregarded the two principles--competition and decentralised information processing through prices--correctly explained in The Wealth of Nations, and promoted incorrect ideas about money and capital, with well-known results.

Regardless of the fact that both classical authors and Karl Marx use the terms money and capital synonymously, the unity of capital and money can be deduced as well from the logic of classical theory.

The classical theorists and Karl Marx, as well as all the tendencies based on these classical concepts, assume that capital will flow automatically to its most profitable use.

This means that if a "capitalist" (actually we should refer to capital, because the "capitalist" does not make any decisions, he is not an entrepreneur) can earn more money in another sector, he will reallocate his capital away from less profitable use to more profitable use, until the profit is the same overall. The idea, for a lot of reasons more of a theoretical concept than something practically feasible, is that capital that could be invested in clothes, for instance, will rather be invested in the housing sector, if the return on investment is higher in the housing sector. That will reduce the supply of clothes and increase the return in the clothing sector as well as increase the supply in the housing sector and lowering the return there, until the profit is the same in both sectors.

In order to be able to do this, capital must be available in its most liquid form: money. It is well possible to start a company, or buy part of one with money, but it is not possible to reallocate capital if it takes the form of an excavator or a harvester. If we talk about reallocation in the context of classical theory, we talk about the reallocation of money, not capital. We will see that this makes a big difference.

Furthermore, in classics theory we have three production factors, labour, capital and land. The price for labour is the wage, the price for capital is the profit and the price for land is the rent.

There is no need to explain in detail the term "economic rent". Whoever is interested in a further explanation of the term can read the article on David Ricardo on www.economics-reloaded.com. What we are interested in here is the fact that remuneration of productive factors, labour, land and capital, depends on their scarcity in relation to demand. It is, nevertheless, a little bit more complicated than this. We can easily understand that work must be paid for, because otherwise a) no one would work and b) very soon there would be no workers.

But it is debatable whether it is necessary to pay for land, and it can be questioned as well whether land is scarce (as the classical authors assumed) or whether the same can be said of water, but we will not discuss this now. We accept the assumption that land must be paid for. (Actually it is completely irrelevant in the context of Keynesian theory whether land is a productive factor or not.)

We accept, therefore, that both land and labour must be paid for. The price of labour is the wage and the price of land is economic rent; and both are understood as prices in the context of a market economy. Wages and economic rent have, therefore, a meaningful function in a market economy; they signal scarcity and they induce the elimination of the scarcity. They are necessary for the allocation of resources.

The adaptation of work to changes in the industrial structure is only possible if there is an incentive for the workforce to qualify for new jobs. If a programmer does not earn more than a butcher, the butcher has no incentive to study informatics. Likewise, a farmer will not abandon his job to work in industry if he cannot make a higher wage there.

An incentive is needed to induce a land owner to sell his land if this land is needed for a plant. He will only sell his land if he earns more money by selling it than what he can earn by cultivating crops.

This seems trivial, but it is something we must understand. Wages and economic rents are equivalent to prices in the context of a market economy. Moreover, these prices contain meaningful information, they signal scarcity and they lead to the reallocation of resources.

Here we have arrived at a crucial point. In classical theory, capital (i.e. money) is considered something scarce. Because it is scarce it has a price (see above). Only those things that are scarce have a price. Air, sun, sand in the desert and so forth have no price because they are not scarce.

Why is capital seen as scarce in classical theory? It is scarce because sacrifices are required to obtain it.

In classical theory, capital is the result of unconsumed income from the past. If people have relinquished consumption in the present in order to consume more in the future, capital is scarce. If a sacrifice is needed to obtain something, the thing is scarce and it can only be obtained if compensation is provided for the sacrifice.

Capital (i.e. money – Adam Smith, Jean Baptiste Say or David Ricarod use the terms as synonyms) therefore has a price in classical theory. So if capital, i.e. money, were scarce, profit would have the function of a price in the sense of a market economy.

If capital were scarce, if it were the result of non-consumed income of the past, the price of capital, the profit, must be high enough to induce people to forego consumption in the present for an increased consumption in the future. Only if the preference for consumption in the present must be compensated by a higher consumption in the future, the relationship must be balanced by a profit on capital.

The higher this price (the profit), the more consumption in the present will be reduced in favour of higher consumption in the future. Future consumption will increase the more profitable investments that were made possible by sacrifice.

At the same time this price would guarantee, if capital were scarce and if the profit were therefore a price in the sense of a market economy, that capital would be allocated in an optimal way, and that it would flow to the most profitable use.

People who relinquish consumption in order to get money for investment purposes, will invest it in the most profitable way.
The crucial point is that capital is a production factor in classical theory and that it is something scarce.

The fatal error of the classical authors and all the tendencies (such as neoliberalism and Marxism) that are based on their ideas is the confusion between capital and money. In other words, in classical theory, money for investment purposes is not-consumed income of the past. Classical authors refer to this as capital, but they actually mean money, and very often the two terms are used synonymously in the same paragraph. This is the beginning of the problem.

If capital is simply money, something that is the case in the context of investments because for investments we need it in the most liquid form (money), no sacrifice is needed to obtain it, and it is not the result of unconsumed income from the past. The amount of money provided by the central banks is merely a political decision which depends on the evaluation of the situation by the relevant central bank.

Money is not scarce per se and, therefore, the price of money--the interest rate--is not a price in the meaning of a market economy. Stated differently, in Keynesian theory the money market is not similar to the market for potatoes or any other market. If potatoes are expensive because demand exceeds supply,

the farmer will grow more potatoes and consumers will reduce their consumption of potatoes (if they have an alternative). The price is a signal of scarcity and the market player reacts to this signal.

The interest rate is not a price in this sense; it does not play a steering role in the allocation of resources. It is true that with high interest rates only those investments that are sufficiently profitable to earn these interest rates will be pursued. The higher the interest rate, the higher the demand for the investment. Nevertheless, the interest rate does not have an allocation function, because a more profitable investment would be able to attract the necessary resources, for instance qualified workers, because it could pay more. Relevant is only the allocation of the scarce resources the interest rates are irrelevant. Interest rates are costs to be paid by the company, but they do not have an effect on the allocation of scarce resources.

It can easily be recognised that money is not a productive factor in the same way as raw materials or qualified workers that are deployed wherever they yield the highest return. The interest rate is not the result of a market process, but depends on the decisions of central banks.

The price of money can be 0.25% as it is these days (in 2015) or 6%; this depends on the Central Bank's evaluation of the economic situation. It will be set high if the central bankers fear inflation, and it will be low in a situation of high unemployment.

More precisely, interest rates only have a steering function in a situation of full employment, something that is always the case for classical theory. With full employment we see a trade-off between the production of goods for consumption and the production of capital goods. In this case, the interest rate has the function of a market price. A high interest rate induces more savings, and whoever saves more, will consume less. The production of consumer goods will therefore decrease, and resources can be re-allocated to the production of capital goods.

At the same time, there will be more money available for investment purposes and those not employed in the consumer goods industry can therefore be employed in the capital goods industry.

This is only meaningful in a situation of full employment. In a situation of full employment, an increase in consumer goods is only possible at the expense of the production of capital goods, and vice versa. This trade-off does not exist in the case of unemployment. In this case, an increase in both areas is possible.

In a situation of unemployment, the interest rate (or the price of money) does not have a steering function, because even without interest rates the more profitable investments will prevail, because they can attract the scarce resources through higher remuneration. However, a high interest rate can impede investment and full employment.

We will not address at the moment the fact that, in reality, it is not the most profitable investment that will prevail, but the one which offers more security. We discuss this topic in more detail on www.economics-reloaded.com.

We have a similar problem with the term "savings" as we have with the term capital (namely, the equating of capital and money and the idea that capital is a production factor). To save, or "to accumulate" in the words of Karl Marx and Jean Baptiste Say, means not to consume income. Savings are the result of unconsumed income from the past. These means can be used for investment purposes and, in turn, the level of investment depends on prior savings. In other words, a prior sacrifice is needed. In Keynesian theory it is the other way round. Investment, this is the relevant statement in the context of Keynesian theory, is a condition for savings and not, as in classical theory, the result of the investment.

It is easy to see why classical theory is wrong. If an entrepreneur wants to realise an expansion investment, for instance if he wants to buy a crane, he can save money first (instead of consuming a part of his income) and then buy it. In this case he would behave in accordance with classical theory, as buying the crane has required a sacrifice in the past.

He can just as well go to a bank and borrow the money. The bank will provide him with a loan and generate this money through scriptural money or by borrowing it from the Central Bank. If the entrepreneur later pays back the loan, the equivalent sum of money will be destroyed. In this case, saving happens in the future. The entrepreneur cannot consume all of his earnings in the future. Saving will happen in the future and prior saving was not needed for the investment, but is the consequence of the investment. Saving has increased because there was a prior investment. The savings necessary to pay back the loan were engendered by the investment, but were not the condition of investment.

We must therefore be precise what we mean by savings. In classical thinking, saving is the non-consumption of income from the past. For Keynes, saving is the non-consumption of income in the future. This is something very different.

If we understand by savings the non-consumption of income of the past, then capital for investment purposes is scarce and requires a sacrifice, and the price for capital, the profit, is a price in the sense of a market economy. To induce someone to make a sacrifice necessitates that there be a compensation for his sacrifice, something that only highly profitable investments can offer.

But if saving is the non-consumption of income of the future, it is not scarce. On the contrary, the more investments, the higher the savings. No sacrifice is required, because without the investments the savings would not have been generated.

If someone earns $10,000 a year more by investing, it is difficult to explain to him that he must make a sacrifice by setting aside $1,000 to pay back a credit. If we follow the logic that we make a sacrifice if part of the increased income is used to pay back a loan, then no one would invest.

From this follows an important consequence. If we consider capital a scarce production factor, investments that cannot generate high interest rates will not be pursued, leading to higher unemployment.

If, for instance, a property must yield a profit of 5% annually because otherwise the mortgage cannot be paid back, fewer properties will be constructed and fewer jobs created than if the properties need only yield 3%.

But if money is not a scarce production factor, the interest rate can be lowered until full employment is achieved.

The classical authors only imagine savings as unconsumed income of the past. They assumed that institutional investors (banks) would only grant a credit if someone else had previously saved money. The truth is that the banking system can generate money. In order to grant a credit, they do not need to depend on prior savings from their customers. Adam Smith recognised this and described similar mechanisms using Scottish banks as an example. However, he was not aware that this fact contradicts the rest of his theories. We address this in more detail on www.economics-reloaded.com.

The classical authors also take it for granted that an increase in savings automatically leads to an increase in investment. This relationship is, however, far less plausible than the opposite scenario of increased investment leading to an increase in savings.

We will see later on that this thesis is no longer true if there is an alternative to consuming, saving and investing, namely, the option to investment in products as liquid as money.

Investments in listed securities are almost as liquid as money itself. They can be bought and sold at any moment. In other words, the decision is reversible at any moment and a decision that is reversible at any moment is not risky. But this kind of investment doesn't generate jobs.

Less problematic is the assumption, more compatible with Keynesian theory, that any investment results in

a saving of the same amount, because entrepreneurs will not invest in something if they do not believe that the savings generated by these investments will allow them to pay back their loan.

Nevertheless, Keynes's critique of classical economic concepts about capital as unconsumed income from the past is more radical.

First, Keynes affirms that capital in the sense of the classical authors is not needed for investments. Capital, in the classical sense (unconsumed income from the past), is at the most a limiting factor for investments in cases of full employment, but it is not a condition for investments.

Second, saving diminishes demand. In the case of unemployment, a further decrease of demand through more savings will lead to an even weaker investment.

With a grain of salt it can be said that classical theory assumes that a restructuring of the economy is easier if interest rates are high. This would be true if interest rates had an impact on allocation, but this is not the case.

To be more concrete: what is currently (in 2015) attempted in Greece, namely a restructuring of the economy through savings, cannot work.

Keynes's third argument is more complex. Savings does not depend on the interest rate, but on income. Keynes's discussion of this issue is much more sophisticated, but we can already see the point if we think of a loan. A loan, at least if used for investment purposes, leads to increased income and, if part of this income is not consumed, to further savings. We reach a new equilibrium if the income increases so much that the loan can be paid back. A high interest rate has the only effect of impeding more investments and that leads to less income than would be possible.

To put it short: In classical theory, high interest rates guarantee that there is enough capital for investments. In Keynesian theory, high interest rates make any investments impossible that are not able to overcome the hurdle of these high interest rates.

The final reason for this is that capital is considered by classical theorists as something scarce and it is not at all seen as scarce in Keynesian theory.

III. Keynesian Theory

It is useful to take a closer look at the title of the book. The name of the book is "General Theory of Employment, Interest and Money". It is pretty clear what a book with this title is about: It is about employment, interest and money. It is necessary to say that, because there are a lot of people who believe that the Keynesian theory is about expansive fiscal policy.

The part of employment we will address later. To summarise: In classical theory the amount of the national product depends on the labour market. In case of unemployment wages have to be lowered until full employment is reached. In classical theory unemployment can only exist if wages are too high. To put it simple: If the wage is a dollar a week, there is no unemployment. It would be cheaper to employ someone to do the laundry than to buy a washing machine.

We have already seen in the chapter about classical theory that in that concept the interest rate is the price for capital and that capital and money is the same thing. Capital is the result of a sacrifice. Money/capital is scarce and has a price.

But if capital is nothing else than money, it is not scarce. It can be printed. The interest rate is therefore not a price in the sense of a market economy. But if the interest rate is not a price in the sense of a market economy, what is it then and what is its function?

In order to understand that, we have to go a little bit further. The interest rate is not formed on the capital market, but on the money market, and this is somewhat different and has little in common with the markets of goods or with the labour market.

Keynes distinguishes three different functions of money. Money is needed for transactions. This money is called transaction cash. It is needed to buy goods. This money is not necessarily in the wallet, you can pay with credit cards as well, but in any case it must be liquid, in other words, it must be a general means of payment which can be transferred from one use to another.

Besides that some people keep some money on their bank account or under the pillow, if they don't trust banks, in order to be prepared for any kind of misfortune. This function is of little relevance in Keynesian theory.

Much more important is the third function of money. Some people keep money for speculative reasons. In this case people consciously relinquish profit. This money might as well be kept on the bank account or under a pillow, as it yields little or no profit.

This behaviour is irrational according to classical theory, where money is spent or saved in order to be invested in something that allows a greater consumption in the future as a compensation for the sacrifice.

If a market player regards an investment too risky, he will, in classical theory, consume the money instead of saving and investing it. He will not invest if he fears that there will be no reward, because there is a preference for consumption in the present.

But in Keynesian theory – and in reality – there is a third possibility. It is possible to invest in listed securities. These are almost as liquid as money, but they yield some return.

Listed securities are secure because the investment decision can be reversed at any moment. Listed securities can be reversed back into money just as fast as money can be transformed into listed securities. In Keynesian theory there is therefore something he calls liquidity preference.

Based on these assumptions Keynes establishes a relationship between interest rates and national product. The reader is referred to www.economics-reloaded.com for more details.

If we assume a certain money supply, the need for transaction cash is low if the national product is low, because there are few transactions of goods. Therefore there is a lot of money not needed for transactions and people have to decide whether they keep it on their bank accounts (or under the pillow), where they get no return at all, or whether they want to invest it in something.

This wouldn't be a big problem if they didn't have the option to invest it on the stock market. Without the stock market, people (actually institutional investors like banks and insurance firms, these are the relevant market players in this sector) would have only two choices: Consumption or investment. Both increase demand and therefore production and employment.

Unfortunately there is a third option: Investing in the stock market. That doesn't create any demand for goods and services and therefore doesn't promote any production and employment.

Real investments are illiquid, the decision for a real investment can't be reversed. A solar desalination plant cannot be reconverted into money without heavy loses. If the results don't agree with expectations, the investor will lose money.

Real investments therefore compete with listed securities and must yield a greater profit than the listed securities with no risk at all – at least if the speculators believe that the price of the securities won't fall. If both investments seem too risky, people will keep their money in speculative funds and relinquish any returns.

The difficult part of Keynesian theory is this: If the national product increases, more money will be needed for transaction purposes. Some holders of securities will be obliged to sell them and therefore the price of securities will fall, their return increase. A dividend of $5 on a security which costs $100 is not much. A dividend of $5 on a security which costs 50 dollars is a lot. This will induce some people to reduce their speculative funds. For some this raise in return will be enough to reduce their speculative funds and invest in the stock market. In other words: The higher the national product, the smaller the speculative fund. This is a little bit complicated. We will return to the topic.

The reason given by Keynes for the liquidity preference is insecurity. This insecurity can be reduced if the decision is reversible, and the more liquid an investment, the easier it can be reversed.

The term insecurity should be specified. Insecurity is the result of a lack of information, and in order to evaluate a real investment much more information is needed. Listed securities are a homogenous product. There is no difference between stocks of a pharmaceutical company and stocks of a company that produces cars. There is no need to know anything about pharmaceuticals or about cars to deal with shares of those companies.

The case of the example mentioned above, the solar-driven desalination plant, is different. A lot of information and knowledge is needed to evaluate the potential profitability and the risks. One must know how much water is actually produced by this plant, how much land can be irrigated with this water, what can be cultivated on this land and what is needed to improve the quality of the soil, what are the market prices of the products and so on. This is something that exceeds the intellectual capacity of institutional investors. That's why they prefer to speculate on the stock markets.

The speculative fund is a term difficult to understand and actually it doesn't change a lot if we eliminate the concept. It is not essential for Keynesian theory, as we will see later on.

In any case it is crystal-clear that the need for money for transactional purposes is low if the national product is low. It is equally obvious that the amount of the speculative fund, which doesn't yield any return if people keep it under the pillow and very little if people keep it on their bank account, is high in this case.

The owners of speculations funds are of different types. Some of them leave the speculative fund even if the interest rates are very low and the price of securities therefore very high. Remember: $5 for a security that costs $100 is not a lot, $5 for a security which costs $100 is a lot. We can assume therefore that those who are most prepared to take risks have already invested in the stock markets, if the national product is low.

If the national product grows, the need for money for transactions increases. Some holders of securities and stocks have to sell them in order to get more money for transaction purposes. The price of them will fall, the return increase. This will induce some of the more worried to invest in the listed securities instead of keeping their money on their bank account.

This will go on until the price of stocks and other listed securities is so low and the return so high that no speculative fund remains.

The conclusion looks classic, but the causal relationship is very different. If the national product is very high and if we reach full employment, the type of interest is high and the stock exchange prices are low.

If there is no speculative fund an increase of the national product can only be obtained by selling securities and in this case there will be no other owners of speculative funds to reduce the effect. The increase of the interest rate will be so strong, that real investments will be no longer possible.

This situation is called the classical situation, although the way Keynes got there is completely different.

What was to be explained? The classical economists actually don't have any monetary theory. They assume, as a lot of people still do nowadays, that money is only used for the purpose of transaction,

that money is only needed to transfer goods. An increase in the amount of money would only lead to an increase of prices, without a change in the relationship of these prices. Money is a pure veil. But we will not discuss these issues here and the reader is referred to www.economics-reloaded.com for a more detailed discussion. Keynes's basic assertion will remain unchanged, although Milton Friedman claims that Keynesian theory is called into question if it is assumed that lenders anticipate inflation.

What should be understood is that: In classical theory full employment is always granted and can always be obtained by a reduction of wages. Interest rates will only determine whether consumer goods or capital goods are produced, because in classical theory capital is a scarce production factor that can only be obtained if a price is paid for that production factor. Unemployment due to a lack of demand is impossible, because production will always be absorbed by consumption or investment.

In Keynesian theory the interest rate is determined by the money market, something inexistent in classical theory, and this money market is a kind of casino. It is in this casino where the demand for investments is determined. More simply put, money, as opposed to capital, something that is not scarce, can impede real investments which would create jobs and increase the national product.

If we look at things in more detail, the situation is still a lot stranger than imagined by Keynes. Minimal return can be enormous if huge volumes of money are transferred. In 2013 alone turnover on the stock markets of the world was $30 trillion. That corresponds to the GPD of the US, China, Germany and Japan put together, and to almost half of global GPD ($70 trillions).

It is much more interesting for institutional investors to invest their money in the stock markets, than lending money to companies for real investments. This, at least in part, is the reason why private banks do not pay any interest on deposits nor give people credit nowadays (2015) – they get money almost for free by the central banks, but they do not pass that on to their customers. Small credits for companies lead to big administrative costs. Transferring huge amounts of money from one place to another (i.e. into listed securities) can be done in seconds.

III.I What is Questioned by Keynes?

Putting aside the two elements mentioned at the beginning characterising market economies, competition and decentralised information processing through prices, all the other elements of the classics are questioned, especially the classic assumption that markets tend towards equilibrium. We abstract from the fact that equilibrium is something very relative in classical thinking. In the work of David Ricardo an equilibrium on the labour market is even achieved if the workers get paid less than what is needed for survive. In this case they die and dead workers are not unemployed. For a further discussion of the theory of David Ricardo see www.economics-reloaded.com.

Let's summarise what was said until now: Savings in classical thinking is capital used for investment purposes, but actually they mean money and not machines, tools, raw materials etc. We can deduce that not only from the fact that they use the terms "money" and "capital" as synonyms, very often inside the same paragraph, but also from the context. Capital is seen as something that can be used for any aim, and this is a characteristic that only money has.

Capital, i.e. money, for investment purposes is the result of a renunciation of consumption in the past, it is therefore the result of sacrifice and it is therefore scarce. Being scarce, it has a price, the interest rate from the point of view of the saver, or the profit from the point of view of the investor. Therefore capital is only disposable if the profit of the entrepreneur is high enough to compensate the saver for his sacrifice.

The problem with this logic is that money is disposable, even without any sacrifice, and this logic is therefore

wrong. Institutional investors like banks or insurance companies don't make any sacrifice to obtain money. They work with the money of others or money printed by the central banks. It depends on the risk if they work with this money or not. The interest rate is therefore the price to be paid to induce them to leave the safe haven of absolute liquidity. It becomes more and more difficult to convince them to leave that safe haven the more complex and insecure the real economy has become.

It is only in the case of full employment that the interest rate has a similar function in Keynesian theory as in classical theory. In a situation of full employment an increase of the national product is only possible at the expense of the production of consumer goods. In this situation an increase of the interest rate is useful. In this situation an incentive to save more and consume less is useful. High interest rates will lead to an increase in savings and to a reduction of consumption. The resources thus freed can be used for the production of capital goods.

That's how we must understand the title of the book: "General Theory of Employment, Interest and Money". Keynes provides a general theory that treats full employment, the situation supposed normal by the classics, as one possible situation among other possible situations.

In the case of unemployment, however, the interest rate is not a price in the sense of a market economy, because capital for investment purposes, in other words money, is not scarce and something that is not scarce cannot have a price.

In case of unemployment a choice between the production of goods for consumption and capital goods is not needed. To the contrary: If consumption decreases, the willingness to invest decreases as well, because the willingness to invest depends on demand.

If capital were really scarce, a price for capital would be useful even in the case of unemployment and at a microeconomic level the interest rate is useful. A single company, household or individual can't create money. They have a certain amount of money and want that money to be invested in the most profitable way. They will give it to the companies who offer them the highest interest rate. At a microeconomic level money is actually something like a productive factor, it is scarce.

From a macroeconomic view the situation is completely different. From a macroeconomic point of view money is not a fixed sum and can be produced in any quantity. It is therefore useless to regard it as a productive factor. Something that is not scarce can be very relevant for production, like the sun rays on which life on earth depends, but nobody would consider it as a production factor, because it exists in an infinitive amount.

What does that mean in practise? Right now, we are still in the year 2015, savers, insurance companies, banks and other institutional investors like pension funds complain that they are "expropriated" by the central banks, who offer money for almost nothing and that it becomes therefore more and more difficult to invest the money saved.

This is their perspective, but it can also be seen in a different way. In case of unemployment there is no reason to keep the money supply artificially small in order to guarantee a good price for money and eliminate the investments that can't pay this price.

The same argument could be put forward by someone who stores water in his bath tub and complains that the government doesn't poison the water in order to make water expensive.

We have therefore a curious situation. Although money is not scarce at all, and the interest rate is not a price in the sense of a market economy, the interest rate can still, due to the speculation of institutional investors, impede the realisation of real investments and keep the economy in a situation of unemployment.

We can even get to a situation – that's what's happening nowadays, we are still in the year 2015 – where flooding the market with more money only leads to a bubble in the stock markets, but has no impact on the real economy. The interest rate decreases, but that has no impact on the interest for loans, because institutional investors prefer to invest in the stock markets.

The interest rate has therefore a completely different function in Keynesian theory than in classical theory.

Most people believe that the interest rate has an allocation function, that the interest rate is something like the price in the sense of a market economy, that it directs resources to the optimal allocation. That is not the case. The more profitable investment can attract the resources through a higher remuneration. The interest rate can even be zero.

Money is not a production factor. The fact that classical theory as well as Marxism believe that capital, i.e. money, is a production factor is the most fatal error of classical theory, which leads to a whole cascade of other errors.

The strange assumption of classical theory that savings is a condition of investment is based on the same error. This is only true in the case of full employment, and only in the case of full employment a distinction between money and capital is not necessary. In case of full employment, where the productive potential is completely exhausted, an increase of investment is only possible when there is a decrease of consumption. In this case it is indeed necessary to reduce consumption in the present, and this is the meaning of saving: a reduction of consumption.

In case of unemployment we have a different situation. In this case saving is even harmful. What is not needed in this situation is a reduction of demand. For an increase of investment no savings is needed in this situation, because there already are idle resources.

If we speak of unemployment, we mean that the real productive potential is not exhausted. The fact that people are unemployed doesn't mean that there is unemployment in the sense of a not-exhausted productive potential. There must be real potential to produce something.

In this situation, unemployement, the type of interest is only an obstacle, because any investment that covers the risk and the administration costs of the banks will create jobs.

Nevertheless it must be granted that the money produced at the moment the loan was granted is eliminated afterwards, when the loan is paid back. This is only possible if the risk is priced in. If an institutional investor grants 10 loans at the amount of 1000 each and one borrower goes bankrupt, the remaining nine have to eliminate the money during the useful life of the investment. Otherwise we would have an eternal increase of the money supply.

Therefore it is clear that savings in the theory of Keynes is something completely different than in classical theory. In Keynesian theory savings means that part of the income induced by investment is not consumed.

If capital and savings don't have the function attributed to them in classical theory, the whole classical theory collapses like a house of cards.

We can illustrate that with any author of classical theory, and we take David Ricardo as an example. We are not presenting this theory in detail here and the reader is referred to the www.economics-reloaded.com for a more detailed presentation.

David Ricardo assumes that workers' wages will never be higher than the subsistence level, but that the value of what they produce exceeds their wages. This added surplus goes into the pockets of the capitalists.

[It is unclear how in a situation of competition a capitalist can set the price high enough to get any added value, and who is going to buy the products if the value produced is higher than the value of the workers' income, but that is not our problem right now.]

The capitalist will use this added surplus to employ still more workers, who produce a still greater added value. The more workers he employs, the greater the demand for food, which will become more and more expensive, because soil is scarce. He must therefore pay higher and higher wages to keep his workers alive and that will reduce his profits until a stationary state is reached.

The problem with this theory, as well as with all the other versions of classical thinking is that the "capitalist" gets money. If he sells his products, he gets money and that money he invests. There is therefore no need to approach the stationary state step by step. It can be reached immediately by printing money. The capitalist could have borrowed the money from the banks.

The capitalist would have been better off enjoying life by consuming the whole added value and to finance all the investments he wanted to realise by credit. He would have been obliged to use part of his income to pay back the credit, but he could have employed a lot more workers.

Obviously the workers could have done that themselves. If a capitalist is only characterised by having capital and has no special qualification, the workers could have done the same thing. They could have gone to the banks and borrow money as well.

Ricardian theory makes only a little bit of sense if we take into account that the awarding of credit depends more on the means to offer securities than on the profitablity of an investment. But here we will not discuss this issue and the reader is referred to the www.economics-reloaded.de.

The same thing applies to Karl Marx. In his thinking we also find a laborious accumulation. This could have been avoided. The "capitalists" could have been expropriated by the central banks as well. That's easier and less time-consuming.

In the logic of the classics investments and therefore a high employment rate are only possible if the capitalists save, and although capital is considered money, it is scarce and an obstacle for investment.

Actually money is not scarce at all and there is no sacrifice needed to obtain it. What is an obstacle for investment is insecurity. The interest rate is a result of insecurity and it this interest rate that is the hurdle investment has to overcome.

Or to say it with the words of Keynes: The interest rate is not the price paid for a sacrifice, there is none, but the price to pay in order to induce investors to leave the safe haven of liquidity.

More simply put, if it were possible to determine with a security of 100% all the investments profitable enough to pay back the credit and the costs of administration plus the price to be paid for the risk, nothing more, because nothing more is needed, there would be no unemployment at all. Due to the worldwide technological gap there are always options for investments which will afterwards allow to eliminate the money created before.

A deeper analysis of the labour market is therefore not needed, because it is not the market for goods that determines the equilibrium of the labour market, but the money market. The market of goods depends on the money market and the labour market depends on the market for goods. This causality is diametrically opposed to the causality assumed by the classics.

To put it simple: If institutional investors, i.e. banks and insurance companies, would invest in real investments instead of speculating on the stock market, and if they were able to identify profitable investments in the sense of the definition given above, we wouldn't have any unemployment.

To summarise all that: The whole classical theory and all the tendencies that are based on these concepts, i.e neoliberalism, ordoliberalism, Austrian School etc., are based on fundamental errors which in turn leads to a cascade of other errors.

For reasons we are going to explain later it is not possible and was never the intention of Keynes to use Keynesian theory to destill some simple recipes allowing to resolve any kind of economic problem. He only mentioned incidentally what conclusions could possibly be drawn from his thoughts.

But Keynesian theory is the basis of any meaningful debate about economic problems.

Bevor we continue we have to clarify one issue. In the discussion above we assumed that the amount of money is fixed. If the national product increases, more money is needed for transaction purposes. Some people will be obliged to sell their securities in order to get money. The price of these securities will fall, their return will increase. This will induce other people to reduce their speculative funds. At the end nobody will have any speculative funds left and a further increase in the national product will lead to such a strong increase in the interest rate that selling securities will no longer be compensated, because there is no speculative fund left, and so no real investment will be able to compete with these interest rates. We have reached the "classical" sector.

Obviously this is only true if the money supply is fixed, something that doesn't agree with reality.

Central banks can for example increase the money supply through an open-market policy. Open-market policy means that central banks buy securities. In this case money flows into the economy and the central bank gets the securities. It depends on the interest rate by which these securities are discounted whether the private banks accept the offer or not.

The monetary transfer mechanisms are the same as the ones mentioned above. Depending on the evaluation of the risks market players will keep their money in the most liquid form possible and invest it in the stock markets. The other option is to invest in real investments, but at the present time, in the year 2015, there is a clear preference for speculative investments on the stock markets.

It is also possible that private banks don't accept the offer of the central banks, because they think that both, the stock market and real investments, are too risky.

However, this possibility is only a theoretical possibility. If banks and other institutional investors don't invest in the stock markets nor in real investments, they lose their commercial basis. They earn money by investing money. If they stop doing that, they are bankrupt.

We have to keep in mind that a decrease in the interest rates has no impact on the allocation of resources, although we read and hear the opposite every day. Money is not a productive factor and therefore the price of money has no influence on the allocation of resources.

III.2 Expansive Fiscal Policy

If you Google "Keynes" you will find thousands of articles that focus on one aspect that in the original work, "The General Theory of Employment, Interest and Money" is nothing but an annotation: Expansive fiscal policy.

The topic of the book can be deduced from the title. A book with the title "General Theory of Employment, Interest and Money" is about employment, interest and money. The concept of money and interest is the basic error of classical thinking, and that's what Keynes refuted. If we refute the hypothesis that capital is scarce, then the labour market doesn't determine the equilibrium on the labour market any longer. Employment depends on the money market. Keynesian theory is a general theory, because it includes one special case, which is assumed by the classics to be the typical case, full employment.

There can be little doubt therefore what Keynesian theory is about, although nobody cares about the title of the book.

If the topic of the book were expansive fiscal policy, it can be assumed that Keynes would have given his book a different title. Expansive fiscal policy is a possible conclusion that can be drawn from this book, but it is not the main topic of the book.

Keynesian theory is not centered around a lack of demand. Lack of demand is only a consequence of the erroneous concepts of classical theory. Lack of demand is the effect of the problem, but not the cause.

Even if it were true that the interest rate leads to a balance of savings (defined as not-consumed income of the past) and to investment, it is irrelevant. Investment depends on money, not on savings, and the profitability of an investment must be higher than the interest rate determined on the money market.

Actually there is another problem with classical thinking not considered by Keynes. Classical theory assumes that capital, not-consumed money of the past, is needed to employ workers. Unemployment can therefore be the result of a lack of capital. The truth is that workers are employed with money.

The first conclusion to be drawn from Keynesian theory is that the interest rate has to be lowered until it only covers administration costs and risk. This would be, as Keynes stated, the death of the functionless rentier. If money is not artificially kept scarce, it loses its value.

The problem that the central bank nowadays, we are still in 2015, fails with this politics could be resolved. The central bank should lend money to private banks only for real investments and not for speculations on the stock markets. This is a much easier way to dry out the casino than the tax on financial transactions so widely discussed in our media.

However this would lead to a problem, which must be taken into account. If shares are offered for the first time, shares make sense. The company gets money it can use for investments and the investor, the shareholder, is not obliged to hold on to the investment forever, because he can sell his shares at any moment. If this option didn't exist, only investors with a long-term perspective could invest.

It is not necessary to believe in the effectiveness of expansive fiscal policy to find Keynesian theory coherent. But it is useful to understand that the problem exists and why it exists. The classics deny even the existence of the problem, and there is no way to resolve a problem when its existence is denied.

Keynes discusses the possibility that insecurity is so big and so widespread that lowering interest rates through expansive monetary policy is possible, but useless, because investors prefer the stock market, or because the banks don't accept the money offered, because they already have too much of it.

In this situation the government has to invest directly, in other words build roads or housing, promote innovative technologies, invest more in education and so on.

A quick Google search will show us thousands of articles affirming that Keynesian theory has failed, because expansive fiscal policy has failed.

This is wrong for two reasons. First, expansive fiscal policy is only an annotation in Keynesian theory, a possible conclusion that can be drawn, but not the essence of Keynesian theory, as we can read everywhere. Second, there is good expansive fiscal policy and bad expansive fiscal policy. Good expansive fiscal policy creates values which can be used for a long time, for instance by investing in the extension of communication networks, or by enhancing the productivity of the economy, or by investing in research and development. Bad fiscal policy, such as social transfers for example, will only finance consumption.

The idea of expansive fiscal policy is simple. We'll assume an ideal scenario, abstracting from any kind of negative effects that we will discuss later.

We assume that 20% of the national product is saved and 80% is consumed. If the government increases its expenditures by $1 million every year, by taking out a loan in this amount, then building contractors, telecommunications companies, universities etc. will receive $1 million between them. These parties will spend 80%, i.e. $640.000. Grocery stores, cinemas, hotels etc. will get these $640.000 for their services and will in turn spend 80% and so on...

This one million pre-financed by the government must be covered in the long run. For simplicity's sake let's assume that the 20% saved are compulsory savings, in other words, taxes. We also assume that the government uses this money to pay back the loan, which actually means that the money is eliminated.

The question therefore is how much the national product must grow to cover the $1 million extra in government expenditures. In the scenario assumed it must be $5 million, because 20% percent of 5 millions is 1 million. The effect that the national product must increase by a multiple of the initial investment is called multiplier by Keynes. (multiplier = initial investment / (1-c), with c as the percentage of the income consumed. In our case 5 millions = 1 million / (1-0.8)).

If we take a closer look at this example, we can see immediately that the multiplier can be zero in reality and that it is well possible that government debt increases. The goods sold by grocery stores and the like came at least in part from foreign countries. At that point part of the initial impulse goes to foreign countries.

If foreign countries can satisfy the demand better and / or cheaper, or if the goods requested are not available in a country, the primary impulse will go to foreign countries. Germany for instance is in the nice position that foreign countries do that. They run into debt in order to buy German products. The problem is that they will not and cannot do that forever.

Furthermore, governmental expenditures will increase the earnings of the companies and the yield on capital, which in turn has an impact on the savings rate. The more unequal the distribution of income, the higher the savings rate and the lower the multiplier effect.

Last but not least there is another problem. If expansive fiscal policy is not supported by an expansive monetary policy, the interest rate will increase. This will not lead to a distortion of allocation, contrary to what we can read everywhere, because the more profitable investment will always be more attractive through a higher remuneration.

However, the government is the most solvent debtor. Therefore it can attract any resources it wants, because it can always pay more. It can for instance create large bureaucracies with qualified people who otherwise would do something productive. We are confronted with a somehow complex problem that we will not address here. The reader is referred to www.economics-reloaded.com.

From what has been said until now we can deduce that an expansive fiscal policy is ineffective in case of structural problems. In this case the government can initiate a flash in the pan, but when the party is over, only liabilities will remain.

If a nation is not competitive, in other words, if it doesn't produce its goods at a competitive price, in an inferior quality or not at all, the initial investment will flow to foreign countries. To continue with our example: If all the food, clothes, electrical appliances come from abroad, the multiplier is zero.

But that doesn't concern Keynes. Remember, expansive fiscal policy is not the central message of his theory. For the sake of analysis Keynes excludes changes in the balance of trade.

Expansive fiscal policy must therefore be looked at in the same perspective as expansive monetary policy. The amount of money has to increase until the interest rate is low enough to reach full employment. However, it must be guaranteed that investments are profitable enough to pay back credit. We can hope to get multiplier effects, but is better if the investment itself can pay back a loan.

Expansive fiscal policy should focus on investments profitable enough to pay back credit. However, there are arguments in favour of expansive fiscal policy.

An increase in government liabilities is acceptable if future generations inherit not only these liabilites, but also assets such as buildings, roads, better education, technological advances and so on. Even if the investments don't pay for themselves during the lifetime of the present generation, it is fair to charge the next generation, if this generation inherits the assets.

However, "inheriting liabilities" is an ambiguous expression in this context. Part of the next generation inherits government bonds, and another part of the next generation inherits the obligation to serve these bonds. What we actually have is a redistribution of money in the next generation. This effect can be reduced, if money isn't kept scarce, the type of interest therefore low.

If expansive monetary policy fails for the reasons given before, a total preference for liquidity which we have today, in 2015, government will be the only market players still able to react, because it is the only one who benefits from all secondary effects.

Investments in research and development are investments in heads. Heads have two legs and can run away. Therefore companies will be very cautious before investing in heads. The government doesn't care about that. Wherever the head goes, unless it doesn't leave the country, it will pay taxes and / or convert its knowledge into marketable products.

It is crucial to see that Keynes discusses only investments. All the other multipliers we find in textbooks about macroeconomics have nothing to do with Keynesian theory, although the opposite is asserted.

(That's by the way the only correct thing of the IS-LM function. The curve is called IS curve, where I = investment and S = savings and C = consumption. If the government increases demand, it should focus on investments. Investments can pay back credit by themselves and they create value and assets that can be transferred to future generations. Consumptive government spending depends on secondary effects, which in a globalised economy flow to foreign countries.)

IV. The IS-LM Model

This part is only interesting for people who deal with economic problems from an academic point of view. We discuss the topic thoroughly, but we have our doubts about their didactic value. It is well plausible that the IS-LM model contributed more to the confusion about Keynesian theory than to actually explaining it.

The IS-LM model is the principle responsible for all the existing confusions about Keynesian theory. The IS-LM model wants to be a representation of Keynesian theory. We never found the original Keynesian theory in textbooks. What we found is the IS-LM model, although this model does not contain the sticking points of Keynesian theory, and is difficult to understand. The only concept people remember after having studied the IS-LM model is expansive fiscal policy, which is actually an annotation of half a page in the original work.

The lack of demand, a problem to be resolved by expansive fiscal policy, is something that most people believe "intuitively" plausible. For most people it is plausible that a lack of demand leads to unemployment.

This generalised "feeling" about a lack of demand is already described by Jean Baptiste Say, for more details see www.economics-reloaded.com. The refutation of this "feeling" given by Jean Baptiste Say is not very convincing, but in any case he correctly described a widespread feeling.

Anyone who has spent at least three semesters studying economics will know the graphic below. It is the famous IS-LM model. If you Google IS-LM model, you get 35 million results. Unfortunately this only shows that the misleading model is widespread, but it doesn't mean that the concept is useful or correct.

The model is presented as neoclassical synthesis, in other words a synthesis between Keynesian theory and neoclassical theory. The truth is that it is impossible to make a synthesis of neoclassical theory and Keynesian theory, because they are incompatible with one other.

This author would say that it is pure neoclassical with very little Keynes. To make a synthesis of two incompatible theories is only possible if central concepts of one of these theories are abandoned. That's what happened in this case.

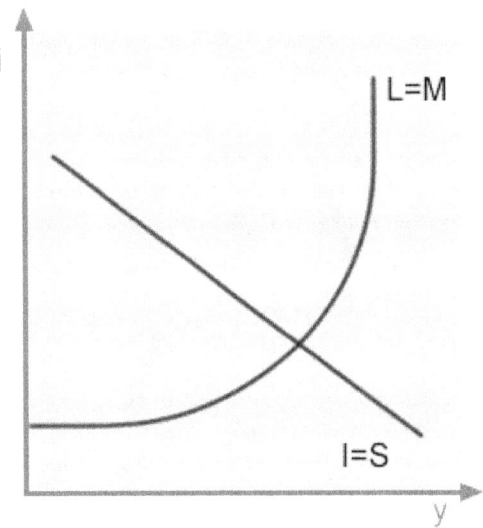

The IS curve is a presentation of all combinations of interest rate (i) and national income (y) where savings and investment are in equilibrium. That also means that the market of goods is in equilibrium. What has not been consumed has been saved by some people and invested by others.

This curve can be interpreted in a Keynesian way and in a neoclassical / classical way, and this is the problem. This curve leads to confusion.

In the Keynesian interpretation savings would FOLLOW investments. This would be an interpretation compatible with Keynesian theory.

Investors calculate with a certain profitability of their projects. That means that the cheaper the credit, the more investments there will be. The more investments, the higher the national income. To get to a new equilibrium, national income must increase until savings, which depend on the national income, are as high as the investments. That means that high interest rates lead to a small national income, because high interest rates lead to fewer investments. [If this is too imprecise for some people, they have to think about the example given above with the "compulsory" savings through taxes or something similar.] The lower the interest rates, the more investments there will be, the more savings is needed and savings depends on the national income. In this logic savings follows investment and the interest rate is a hurdle to overcome, and not an incentive for saving.

Nevertheless there is a little problem with this curve. The equilibriums described are reached EX POST. They describe different combinations of interest rates and national income levels where investments equal savings, but they don't describe how to get from one equilibrium to the other. This is no problem if we only consider the equilibrium as the result of a process, but it becomes a problem if we want to know how to get there.

In textbooks we always find the example of an increase of the aggregate demand through an increase of government spending. That moves the IS curve to the right. But then the question is how the IS curve can be moved to the right without money. If the government wants to increase public demand, the amount of money must be increased. That's the reason why this IS curve, in this interpretation, looks Keynesian, but it is not. Investment is financed with money. Money is not scarce in Keynesian theory, but one must have it.

There is a second error with the IS curve. Savings can only be understood in a real context, in other words as non-consumption and therefore a reduction of consumer goods in favour of capital goods. But if the IS curve is moved to the right, there is an idle production potential, otherwise the curve can't be moved to the right. But if there is any productive potential, saving in the sense of the classics is not needed. What is needed is money and that money must be afterwards destroyed when the credit is payed back, otherwise the amount of money would increase indefinitely.

The problem is that saving addresses real relationships. Saving is the opposite of consumption. This is useful, if there is no productive potential left to produce consumer goods. If the only effect of an increase in demand would be an increase in prices, people better save their money. But in a situation of unemployment, where consumer goods can be produced, saving is counterproductive. It is only necessary to pay back the credit.

The IS curve mixes two different levels, the level of the real economy and the monetary level, and the result is nonsense. At the monetary level there is only need for money if we have any idle productive potential. This is not included in the IS curve. What we have is savings, but that's not what we need.

Understood as a description of equilibriums the curve makes sense. But without money, we can't move it to the right, as any textbook about macroeconomics will tell you.

This would be the classical interpretation, which is compatible with the ideas of Adam Smith, David Ricardo or Jean Baptiste Say. This interpretation has nothing to do with Keynes, but in this case there is no mix-up between the real level of the economy and the monetary level. The classics would have put some MONEY to the side, because actually only MONEY can be invested. Savings in this sense means not-consumed income of the past, in the form of MONEY. This concept is wrong, because for investment there is no need for MONEY in the form of not-consumed income of the past. Savings can only be defined in real terms. Savings is the production of consumer goods instead of capital goods.

Under these false assumptions the IS curve would show that if national income is low (the population must be considered invariable in this case), the national income is just high enough to buy daily goods and there is little savings. Capital is therefore scarce, the interest rate is high. This is necessary, because in this case saving really requires sacrifice. Savings can be interpreted in this case at a real level. If the productivity is low, all the productive potential is needed to produce daily goods. The production of capital goods, which improves investments, requires sacrifice.

Producing more capital goods is only possible if people reduce their already low consumption. On the other hand investments are highly profitable, because an increase in the productive potential is highly profitable, because there is strong demand.

If national income increases, and if we suppose that there is no increase in the population, the sacrifice is lower and only a lower interest rate is needed to induce people to save more. On the other hand products can only be sold at a lower price, and profit is therefore lower.

The classical interpretation would be more coherent in terms of logic, the money to invest would be there, but this interpretation has nothing to do with Keynes. The Keynesian interpretation would be Keynes, but this interpretation doesn't take into account money and it doesn't work. To put it short: The IS-LM model is nonsense.

The very name, IS curve, I = investment and S = saving is already misleading, because saving, in the

classical sense, is not needed and the main point is missing. The main point of Keynesian theory is how investments are financed and they are financed with money, and money is not scarce.

Savings can only interpreted as a meaningful term at the level of the real economy. Savings is needed if consumption exceeds the productive potential. In this case capital goods, which improve productivity, can only be produced by saving.

The IS-LM model mixes to different levels, the monetary level and the real economy level.

In the IS curve we have no money, and it can therefore only be interpreted in the classical sense.

If savings is the condition for investment, that's what the classics believe, then the capital for investment purposes is scarce and scarce goods have a price, in this case the interest rate. In this case only the most profitable investments will be realised, and others, even if they created jobs, will not be realised. The lack of capital for investments can lead to unemployment. The problem is that this scenario excludes the possibility of a right shift of the IS curve. If the government can move the IS curve to the right, there was an idle productive potential, otherwise it wouldn't have been possible to move it to the right by increasing aggregate demand.

The heart of Keynesian theory is the opposite. The capital for investment purposes is not scarce. For the production of capital, i.e. money, no sacrifice is needed. Actually not even savings is needed. The heart of Keynesian theory is that the interest rate is not the incentive needed to induce people to create capital and to save. In a situation of unemployment the interest rate is only a hurdle to overcome with no real function in a market economy.

The heart of Keynesian theory is not only not included in the IS curve, but the IS curve suggests the opposite of Keynesian theory. Investments are financed with money, not with savings.

It is not possible to interpret the model in the sense of Keynes by saying that in Keynesian theory savings depends on national income, because this is irrelevant and is true in both situations. In the classical version, where part of the income of the past has been saved and in the Keynesian version, were people will save in the future to pay back their credit. The model doesn't become more correct by saying that savings depends on income, because that is not the central point. The crucial point is that in Keynesian theory investments depends on money, not on savings.

The LM curve on the other hand shows all the combinations of interest rates and national income, where the money market is in equilibrium, in other words, where the demand for money is equal the supply for money. This means that the return you get by buying a security determines how much money people will keep in their bank account for (almost) no return.

How we define the speculative fund doesn't matter. Realistically speaking the speculative fund can be seen as the money held in bank accounts for almost no return, or less realistically, as the money people keep under their pillows, with no return at all.

To put it simple: If the return on a security is 15% percent, nobody keeps money in his bank account. If the return is 5%, percent and if everybody expects that the value of securities will fall, people will prefer to keep their money in their bank accounts. It is to assume that the reader of these lines has a strong preference for liquidity, but it is clear that for the reader of these lines as well as for the general public, there is a return where he will withdraw his money from his bank accounts and buy securities. Then the money market is in equilibrium.

If the national income is low, the need for money for transaction purposes is low, because few goods are exchanged. If the amount of money is given, the speculative fund is high.

In the speculative fund we have a wide range of risk aversion or, as it is called by Keynes, preference for liquidity. This is how Keynes calls it, because liquidity means security. The risk is low if an investment can be reconverted at any moment to the most liquid form, money. Listed securities are therefore a very secure investment, because they can be reconverted at any moment into this most liquid form.

Therefore the speculative fund is held by people who need very high interest rates to be induced to take money out of their bank accounts, where they get no return at all, and to invest it in the stock market, and there are those who will do that as soon as the interest rate gets below a certain level.

If the national income is low, the amount of money needed for transaction purposes is low as well, and the speculative fund is high. We can therefore assume that all people with low risk aversion have left the safe haven of liquidity and have invested in the stock market. Quoted share prices are therefore high and the return on these securities low.

(We remember, see above: $5 for a security that costs $100 is not a lot. $5 for a security that costs $50 is a lot.)

If the national income increases some people will have to sell securities in order to get the money for transaction purposes. The quoted share prices will fall, the return will increase. This will induce some people to buy securities who have so far remained in the safe haven of liquidity.

This point is a little bit complicated: We can imagine that some people with a high risk tolerance will sell, because they are obliged to. In isolation this effect will lead to a price decrease for the quoted share. On the other hand less risk-tolerant market players will buy them, and that will raise the share price. But in total the share price will go down and the return will go up.

In the end, if the national income increases more and more, a point will be reached were no speculative funds are left. Even the less risk-tolerant will leave the safe haven of liquidity if the potential returns are, say, 30%.

[We can also imagine something different, if we want. If the return for securities is low, only few people will make the effort needed to inform themselves how the stock markets work. But if they can earn a lot of money, they will do it.]

At this point the national income can't increase anymore if the central bank doesn't increase the money supply, because there will be no compensation effect if people sell securities once there are no speculative funds left. If in this situation the central bank doesn't increase the money supply, any increase of national income will increase the interest rates on the MONEY MARKET, which will make it more and more difficult for real investments. If people can get a return from a liquid security with almost no risk, then the return on a risky real investment must be higher.

The higher the national income, the lower the speculative fund, the lower the share price, the higher the interest rate on the money market, the more difficult it becomes for real investments to compete with the stock market.

Textbooks about macroeconomics distinguish three sections of the LM curve. The liquidity trap, where an increase in national income has no impact on interest rates, the section where an increase in the national income leads two an increase of the interest rates, but an increase in national income is possible and the classical sector, where any further increase of the national income is impossible, because the raise of the interest rates would be so high, that no more investments are possible.

The explanation for the liquidity trap in most textbooks is nonsense. It is argued that more money would tacitly be put in the speculative fund and therefore wouldn't have any impact on interest rates. This is

nonsense. In the liquidity trap it will be impossible to inject more money into the market, because nobody needs it. People will not increase their speculative funds with more money they would have to pay for, if they have no idea what to do with this money. They will simply not accept it.

Institutional investors will not accept more money from the central bank because they already have more money than they need. They will not borrow money from the central bank and pay and interest rates if the only use they have for this money is to put in the speculative fund where they get no return at all. The speculative fund is only interesting for money still in circulation.

What we really see nowadays, we are still in the year 2015, is something different. Institutional investors take the money, but invest it in the stock market, which leads to an increase in stock prices. The interest rate continues to go down, but we don't see that this has an impact on the real economy.

The point is that institutional investors have to do something with money, because they earn money with money. If they stop taking the money offered to them by the central banks, they go bankrupt.

The sector where an increase of the national income is no longer possible because it would require to sell securities with the effect that real investments would be displaced is called the classical sector in textbooks about macroeconomics.

This logic would be true, if money were capital in the sense of the classics, i.e. if it were not consumed income of the past, if capital were a scarce production factor. But money is not a productive factor and first and foremost it is not scarce.

In a situation of unemployment we will never see a classical sector in reality. (Unemployment is defined here as idle productive resources.) If there are idle productive resources, the central bank will never keep the money supply low, unless they fear what Keynes calls bottle necks. If the idle productive resources depend on other scarce resources, there is no way to use them, but in a globalised economy that never happens.

The term classical sector suggests that we have full employment. This is not true for capital, if by capital we mean money, and it is not true for labour. Capital in the sense of money is never scarce, and the LM curve doesn't allow for any conclusions about labour. Even in the classical sector unemployment on the labour market is possible.

It is true that in a classical situation of full employment more money would only lead to inflation and inflation to higher interest rates, because lenders will anticipate inflation, but the idea that we get to a classic situation by keeping the amount of money scarce is not only misleading, but it is contrary to the conclusions to be drawn from Keynesian theory. If we accept this interpretation, the central banks can reach this classic situation at any level.

What Keynes actually said is that the amount of money must be increased until we get to full employment. The interest rate has to be lowered until there are sufficient investments to get to full employment. Beyond full employment, lowering interest rates is useless, because we would reach a situation where an increase in investment would only lead to inflation.

The LM curve could be interpreted in a different way, but that wouldn't change anything in Keynesian theory: The money market dominates the goods market and the goods market dominates the labour market. We get to the same conclusion without a speculative fund.

The argument starts at the same point as before with speculative funds. If national income is low, there is only little need for money for transaction purposes. There is therefore a lot of "surplus" money that wants to be invested somewhere. There is therefore a big supply of money, and for money the same thing is true as for potatoes. If supply exceeds demand, the price, in the case of money the interest rate, is low. No matter whether it is invested in real investments or in the stock market, it can only be invested at a small return.

The economy will reach a point where there is no money left for investment purposes. Beyond this point any attempt to increase the national income will only lead to an increase of the interest rate with the result that new investments can only be realised at the expense of other investments. We have reached a "classic" situation, if the central bank keeps money scarce, where money is a production factor.

If we want to put it in more real economic terms: Money becomes scarce in this situation if the more profitable investment can really replace the less profitable one. (If money is kept scarce by the central banks.)

The problem with that interpretation would be that the "surplus" of money would in any case have an impact on demand. If people invest it in the stock market, the type of interest would decrease and that would have an impact on real investments. If it is invested directly in a real investment, it would have a direct impact on demand.

If we stick to the original Keynesian theory, a situation is possible where the "surplus" of money doesn't have any impact. If stock prices are very high, the return would therefore be very low, and so people will keep their money in the speculative fund. They do that firstly because the return is too low to induce them to leave the safe haven of securities, and secondly because they fear that the exchange rate will decrease and they will lose money. In this case people will keep their money in a way which yields them no return at all, but where is at least safe.

The difference between these two interpretations is, with or without a speculative fund, that in the first case it can be explained that money has no impact at all on the economy. In the second case there is always an impact, directly or indirectly.

That doesn't change the central message of Keynes. That central message is that the interest rate which is determined in an arbitrary way on the money market, which actually is something like a casino, that this interest rate determines the hurdle real investments have to overcome. To put it more clearly: The labour market depends on a casino.

The Keynesian version, with its concept of speculative funds, explains why people keep money in their current accounts where they get (almost) no return.

[We find it important to mention that the term insecurity, the reason for the liquidity preference, could be stated more precisely. Insecurity is a problem of a lack of information that doesn't allow potential investors to find out about profitable real investments. For the sake of simplicity Keynes explicitly excluded these kinds of problems from his analysis. In the opinion of this author this is a problem that should be addressed.]

As far as institutional investors are concerned speculative funds are less important. They will not increase their speculative fund by borrowing money from the central banks. They will not pay for money, if they don't get a return from this money.

The main thesis remains unchanged: The money market dominates the goods markets.

What we see at the moment, we are still in 2015, is that institutional investors take any amount of money offered to them by the central banks to speculate in the stock markets. The return on these papers, the dividends which determine their interior value is decreasing. Institutional investors speculate on the stock price. The speculation is on the value of the securities, not on the dividend. The interest rate for which the banks lend money will not decrease.

For institutional investors and similar institutions such as hedge funds the casino is more interesting than the real economy. This is always true. We are not going to discuss monetarism here. Monetarism argues with the same monetary transmission mechanism as Keynes, but it assumes that an increase in the money

supply will lead to inflation. The reader can try to find out himself what would happen then. For further information about monetarism the reader is referred to the www.economics-reloaded.com.

Monetarism can't undermine the basic claim of Keynesianism. Monetarism assumes that an increase in public demand will lead to inflation. Inflation would lead to a higher demand for money for transaction purposes. This will lead to a raise in interest rates. The problem is that we have not had any inflation for 30 years, and it is very improbable in a globalised economy that inflation can be induced by an increase of demand, because in a global economy almost any demand can be satisfied with the existing productive potential. Inflation can only occur if it is driven by the cost side, for instance by rising prices for raw materials.

The problem is not inflation, the problem is the indebtedness of the states, as pointed out in chapter III.

In any textbook anywhere in the world Keynesian theory is taught about macroeconomics on the basis of the IS-LM model. It is asserted that this model is a correct interpretation of Keynesian theory or a neoclassical synthesis. This can be questioned. With some effort we can interpret the IS-LM model in a Keynesian way, but the original text is easier to understand.

We expect from models that they simplify reality maintaining the relevant aspects of a certain problem. A roadmap will not show how much the people earn who live in a certain area. This is irrelevant for a driver, but a road map will show the roads.

But if it is easier to observe reality directly than through a model, the model is not needed.

The model suggests a relationship between savings and investment on the one hand, and the money market on the other, whereby the causal relationships are unclear.

If the IS curve is moved to the right through an increase in public spending, one of the typical scenarios discussed in textbooks, national income increases and interest rates, at least in the sectors outside the liquidity trap, will increase.

The same could be achieved by increasing the money supply, which moves the LM curve to the right. That's the other typical case we find in any textbook. If the interest rate is lowered, the LM curve crosses the IS curve at a lower interest rate and national income is higher.

However the IS-LM model describes the casual relationships in a wrong way, which makes it difficult to understand this model.

If government spending should be increased, in other words, if the IS curve should be moved to the right, it is not savings that is needed, as the IS curve suggests, but money. The government issues, for instance, government bonds to finance its expansive fiscal policy.

If the amount of money is fixed, new securities will only be accepted if the old ones were sold. Their share price decreases, their return increases. (For explanations see above.)

This will induce some holders of speculative funds to buy securities. Money is transferred from the idle speculative fund to the government, who will actually use it for stimulating demand.

The result is similar to what we found as an explanation for the LM curve in macroeconomics textbooks, but the causal relationship is different.

The increase of the interest rates is a necessary condition for expansive fiscal policy, otherwise the government wouldn't get the money needed, but not the result.

The interest rate doesn't increase because national income increases, as suggested by the LM curve. It increases, because investment increases. An increase of investment is only possible if the idle money in the speculative fund is transferred to the government, and this can only happen if the interest rate increases.

The IS-LM Model suggests that there are two different options to increase national income and to increase employment: Expansive fiscal policy and/or expansive monetary policy.

That is nonsense. In both cases more money is required, but not capital. An increase in the aggregate demand through an increase in public spending is only possible if the idle money in the speculative fund is transferred to the government or if it is transferred to real investments that are so profitable that they beat the returns from the stock market.

The LM curve suggests that money can be injected by the central banks alone. That is not possible either. The central banks can only inject money if someone wants to have it.

Sentences like "if the government increases the aggregate demand now, the IS curve will shift to the right" are nonsense. Without money the IS curve doesn't shift at all.

[Insertion: Why do macroeconomics textbooks say the IS curve shifts to the right if there is an increase in public demand? To understand that it is necessary to remember how the course of the IS curve is explained: The interest rate, for which money can be borrowed is fixed. If it is high, there are only small investments, because only very few investments are able to overcome this hurdle. The national income needed to provide the necessary savings, and savings depends on income, is therefore low as well. The lower the interest rates, the higher the investments, the higher the national income necessary to generate the corresponding savings. But if the government increases public demand, we don't have a movement along the IS curve. We have more investment at the same interest rate. The curve moves to the right, at least in theory. In practise it doesn't work. If it wants to invest, the government needs money. That saving increases until the amount of savings equals the amount of investment, the explanation above might be true, but that is not the interesting point. The interesting point is that the money needed to finance fiscal policy must be eliminated afterwards.

In a similar way we can deduce the right shift of the LM curve: If the amount of money is high, the speculative fund is high. The market participants who are most prepared to take risks will have bought listed securities. Share prices are therefore high, the return low. If national income increases, some of these high-risk investors will be obliged to sell their securities in order to get money for transaction purposes. This will induce some owners of the idle speculative fund to invest in listed securities, which will partly compensate the effect, but on average the holders of securities will be less willing to take risks, and therefore the return must increase in order to induce them to leave the safe haven of liquidity. This goes on until there is no speculative fund left. If the the central bank increases the supply for money, the LM curve moves to the right, because the speculative fund increases. The problem is that sentences like "if the central bank increases the money supply the LM curve moves to the right" are nonsense. The central bank can offer money, but it depends on the demand for money whether this money is actually bought, not on the supply. No farmer can decide autonomously how many potatoes he wants to sell, and neither can the central bank decide autonomously how much money it wants to supply. Institutional investors will not accept the money offered to them just to increase their speculative fund. That doesn't change anything in Keynesian theory, but the IS-LM model is nonsense. It is still true that institutional investors, especially banks, will accept the money, even if they only use it to speculate on the stock markets. The interest rate is low right now, we are still in 2015, near to zero in fact, but the spark doesn't leap to the real economy where the jobs are created. The money market dominates the goods markets, this is the main message of Keynesian theory, and that is what we see right now. The European Central Bank injects more and more money into the market, but that has only driven up stock prices and has had no impact on the economy.]

The real problem is obscured by the IS-LM model. The lack of demand is only an effect of the preference for liquidity, but not the cause. The problem to be resolved through an expansive fiscal policy or through an expansive monetary policy is the same in both cases. The problem to be resolved in both cases is the same.

The real difference is this: In the case of expansive fiscal policy the government redirects idle money to a productive use, and in the case of expansive monetary policy the interest rate determined by the money market is too high and must be lowered.

In both cases "saving", actually the destruction of money, follows investments. The lack of demand is only an effect of the preference for liquidity, but not the cause of the problem.

The difference between expansive fiscal policy and expansive monetary policy is a different one. The government can invest directly in case of a total preference for liquidity. The risks of this policy have been described in III.2. But money, not savings, is needed to do that. With ex-ante saving, as suggested by the IS curve, the IS curve can't be moved to the right.

The IS curve describes situations where the goods market is in equilibrium, in other words, where savings equals investments, but it does not explain how to get from one equilibrium to another. The interest rate, as explained above, is considered an exogenous variable. The truth is that the interest rate depends on the money supply.

In both cases investment induces more income, and the more income, the more corresponding savings.

The impression that we have two different effects is due to the fact that in the case of the IS curve the government is able to move the IS curve to the right without money. That only works in the world of Harry Potter.

In the case of expansive monetary policy a distorted allocation is impossible, because only the price for money is reduced, but money is not a productive factor. The most profitable investments can attract the really scarce resources whatever the price for money.

The case of expansive fiscal policy is different. Due to the fact that the government is always the most solvent borrower, it can produce whatever it wants and kick out private companies.

Classical economics and the Austrian School see that in a different way, they assume that capital is scarce and a production factor, and therefore they assume that the interest rate is a price in the sense of the market economy, but they are wrong. Their problem is that they don't distinguish very well between capital and money and the IS curve suggests that capital in the sense of non-consumed income of the past is needed. That is not very helpful, and it is the one reason why a lot of people don't understand the difference between classical theory and Keynesian theory.

To repeat: Whether we say "capital" or "money" doesn't make a big difference only if there is full employment. In the case of full employment there are no idle resources which can be activated with money. If more money is injected into the economy in the case of full employment, the only effect would be a raise of inflation. In this case we really need capital, saved income from the past, to extend the productive potential. Saving means not to consume. Savings would therefore lead to a reduction of consumption and the resources used before to produce consumer products can be used to produce capital goods and with these capital goods more consumer goods can be produced in the future.

Only in the case of full employment do we have to address the problem of optimal allocation. (If someone has nothing to do, the question what is to be done first is irrelevant. He can do whatever he wants and whatever must be done. The problem only arises if time becomes scarce.)

In a case of full employment money has an impact on the allocation of resources. Whoever has the money can attract the resources. This is useful, because there is a trade-off between the different uses of money. In the case of unemployment, the lack of money only impedes idle resources to be used in a productive way.

In the special case of full employment classical theory and Keynesian theory arrive at the same results.

Savings is needed to reduce consumption.

In the case of unemployment, and we mean by unemployment the existence of an idle productive potential, and not just unemployment, the two theories are incompatible. That's the reason why Keynes called his book "General Theory on Employment, Interest and Money". It is a theory that includes the special situation assumed by the classics as the normal situation.

When the course of the IS curve is explained in textbooks we can read sentences like this one: "In order to have an equilibrium on the market for goods, savings must equal investments. This saving can only be obtained at a given savings rate, if there is a corresponding volume of national income."

This is correct, as illustrated by the example above. If the savings rate is 20%, then 20% percent of national income is saved. If an investment is $1000, a national income of $5000 dollars is needed. 20% of 5000 = 1000.

Unfortunately we can not deduce from the IS curve where this $1000 should come from. The IS curve is misleading, and it is a misinterpretation of Keynesian theory. In order to invest we FIRST need the money and AFTERWARDS this money is saved or eliminated again. The IS curve, in a Keynesian interpretation, sets the interest rate as an exogenous parameter. That's nonsense. The interest rate depends on the amount of money in circulation.

If the $1000 came from non-consumed income of the past, we have a classical interpretation and all the problems which follow from that. Then money is a productive factor, has a price and is scarce. None of this is true.

If the $1000 will be paid back in the future, we need an explanation where they come from. If they were printed, we don't need savings, in short, the main message of Keynesian theory is not only not included in the IS-LM model, but the IS-LM model is misleading. The IS-LM model describes equilibriums, but the really interesting question is how to get from one equilibrium to the other.

The main message of Keynes can be described in a much more straightforward way. Due to the complexity of the real world, investors find it difficult to detect profitable real investments. That leads to a preference for liquidity. In other words, real investments compete with securities. Classical theory assumes that finding real investments is no problem, and that the main problem is a lack of capital. Keynesian theory, more realistically, assumes that finding profitable real investment is the problem, and capital is no problem at all. There are two different ways, in Keynesian theory, to resolve that problem: by lowering the interest rate, that way lowering the hurdle real investment has to overcome. Another option is direct government investment, if the liquidity preference is so high that even an interest rate of zero wouldn't induce enough investment to reach full employment.

Besides the errors mentioned above, there are other errors or misleading concepts, the crowding-out effect for example, which is discussed extensively in most modern textbooks on macroeconomics: An increase in public spending will move the IS curve to the right, and that will lead to an increase of the interest rate through the monetary transmission mechanism mentioned before and so to a decrease of private investments. In other words: Government spending will kick out private investments. The problem is that this concept doesn't make any sense in Keynesian theory. Why should the central banks restrict the amount of money, even before the economy has reached full employment?

There may be a reason for the central banks to do that, for instance if some bottlenecks impede the economy from growing further and from making use of idle productive factors. In this case more economic growth can only be reached by accepting higher inflation, because higher inflation helps to eliminate bottlenecks, but the central bank may have some reasons to contain inflation.

But in this case the problem is not, as suggested by the crowding-out effect in the context of the IS-LM model, an increase in the interest rate, but a structural problem in the real economy.

With the crowding-out effect the IS-LM model returns to classical thinking. Money is a productive factor and can be scarce. In Keynesian theory money is not a productive factor, it is not capital, it is never scarce, and therefore it has no price in the sense of a market economy.

To summarise: The IS-LM model is something between confusing and wrong, a strange mix between the monetary level and the real level. It induces a mechanical thinking that has nothing to do with reality, a way of thinking considered fatal by Keynes. People move the IS and LM curves from the left to the right and from the right to the left without understanding what they are doing and afterwards they wonder why reality is not as simple as it seems to be on paper.

We don't need models which obscure reality instead of clarifying it and which are irrelevant for explaining reality. It would be better to eliminate the IS-LM model from the textbooks completely.

V. Summary

We can read and hear a lot of nonsense about economics issues every day, but there is no economist on earth about whom we can read and hear so much nonsense as we read and hear about Keynes.

The basic problem is that in most public debates Keynes is reduced to expansive fiscal policy. Expansive fiscal policy is a possible conclusion to be drawn from Keynesian theory, but not the main point. The message is not the lack of demand, because the lack of demand is only the effect, and not the cause.

The main message of Keynesian theory is a complete refutation of the classical concepts about capital, money, interest rates and saving.

Keynes is not a cyclical theorist as we can read everywhere. In Keynesian theory an economy can remain in a situation of unemployment forever, and unlike classical theory Keynes does not assume that there are any automatic mechanisms that bring it back to equilibrium at least in the long run.

If we reduce Keynesianism to expansive fiscal policy, in other words, if Keynesian theory is not understood, we come to the conclusion that Keynesianism is proved wrong if expansive fiscal policy doesn't work. That happened for instance in the Seventies, when an external shock, the increase of the oil price, lead to inflation. For the sake of simplicity Keynes explicitly excludes external shocks from his analyses. We are not going to discuss this situation here, but it is pretty clear that it was a different kind of scenario than the one addressed by Keynesian theory.

In a similar way today's problems in Greece, we are still in 2015, can't be considered as a failure of Keynesian theory, because Keynes never alleged that an increase in public spending can lead an economy out of unemployment if the increase in aggregate demand initiated by an increase of public investment is satisfied in foreign countries.

Keynesian theory cannot be refuted by interpreting Keynes in a misleading way and by alleging afterwards that the misleading interpretation doesn't agree with reality. If we argue that way any economic theory is wrong.

The most serious opponent of Keynesianism is monetarism. Monetarism is a special case. The Keynesian monetary transfer mechanism is accepted, but due to some other assumptions monetarism arrived at the same results as classical theory. Money doesn't matter. (More famous is 'money matters', but this refers to the interpretation of Milton Friedman of the crisis of 1929.) Monetarism assumes that any attempt to increase

national income, whether through an increase in public spending or through lowering the interest rate, will lead to inflation and the higher prices requires an increase in the money neede for transaction purposes. The implicit assumption is that economies tend to full employment, as asserted in classical theory. This way he gets to the same results as classic theory, although the argument is completely different. For a more detailed discussion the reader is referred to www.economics-reloaded.com.

In "General Theory of Employment, Interest and Money" Keynes himself has warned against the mechanical application of his theory, as it is presented in the IS-LM model. For details the reader is referred to the www.economics-reloaded.com. But that didn't help, because nobody reads the book.

Keynesian theory is without any doubt right. Savings is not a condition for investment, nor is sacrifice required to obtain capital, i.e. money, nor is it possible to transfer consumption to the future by saving. Capital is not a scarce product and has therefore no price in the sense of a market economy.

For the same reasons Keynes is the founder of macroeconomics. For the individual market players, the entrepreneurs and the households, everything is true that is not true at all at a macroeconomic level. Households and entrepreneurs can't produce capital, i.e. money, and therefore for them capital is scarce and has a price in the sense of a market economy. For the individual market player saving does make sense.

But if all of them save, the incentive for investment will decrease. We often hear and read that microeconomics focuses on the single market player, macroeconomics on aggregated amounts. That's not really the point. Microeconomics studies rational behaviour from the perspective of an individual market player, but rational behaviour on a microeconomic level can be very irrational at a macroeconomic level.

The classics assume that the interests of individual market players agree with the interests of society as a whole. That is sometimes true, as pointed out in chapter II, and sometimes it is not. It is hard to see, for instance, why investors should be induced to invest if people save more and consume less.

In classical theory savings is the condition for investment, because without savings there is no capital. Capital is scarce. In Keynesian theory capital is not needed for investments. What is needed is money.

For the individual market player the allocation of his capital is an issue as well. He will invest his money in a way that yields him the highest return. From a macroeconomic perspective things are different. Due to the fact that money is not scarce, there is no need to impede less profitable investments. Any investment that is able to pay back the credit, the administration costs of the bank and the risk is useful.

Keynesian theory allows us to see that many ideas we take for granted are actually wrong and will not work. In many countries for instance the pension system is based at least in part on individual capital accumulation. The idea is that the individuals save money during their working lives and will pay for their living with this money once they retire. That doesn't work for a lot of reasons, but especially it will not work if central banks flood the markets with money as they do today. We are still in 2015.

Only in the case that central banks keep the money supply at a low level, money can be earned with money, but that means that the central banks would accept unemployment in order to keep the return on money high. It is obvious that they won't do that.

It is not possible to prepare for an unknown consumption in an unknown future. That is the idea of saving. People save now, investors can take this savings to invest in plants which will produce the unknown consumer goods in an unknown future. They won't do that. If they realise that consumption decreases today, they will not invest at all.

Only in the case that consumed goods are the same in the future as in the present, as is the case with housing, they will invest, but in this case it is not savings that is needed, but money and low interest rates.

However, present times show us that it is difficult, as Keynes already stated, to induce institutional investors, banks and insurance companies or private international intermediaries like hedge funds to leave the casino of the stock markets.

One possibility would be that central banks only provide money to private banks if they in turn convert this money into real investments.

Keynesian theory shows us as well that the famous microcredits are nothing revolutionary. They can have an impact as far as they sharpen social control over the borrowers, and that leads to a more efficient use of resources. But they don't provide capital in the sense of the classics, because what the peasant gets is money and money is not a productive factor, nor is it scarce. At most it is kept scarce. If we abstract from the effects of social control the respective central banks could have printed this money. It doesn't matter if the money is the result of non-consumed income of the past or if it is destroyed afterwards when the credit is paid back.

Equally wrong are all kinds of growth theories, such as the Cobb-Douglas function, which argues with capital as a production factor. If the know-how is there, credit will be paid back, regardless of where the money comes from. If the know-how is not there, it won't be paid back in either case. The only difference is that in the first case, if the money provided for investment purposes is the result of non-consumed income of the past, there is no increase in the money supply in case that the credit is not paid back. In the second case, if the money is just printed, the money supply will increase if the credit is not paid back.

It also happens that Keynesian theory is confronted with undisguised hatred. These people don't understand Keynesian theory, but they understand very well that Keynesianism doesn't agree with their interests.

In classic economics there are three productive factors which must be remunerated, capital with profit, labour with wages and land with rent. It is obvious that remuneration is only possible if these productive factors are scarce. Sunlight for instance is without any doubt a productive factor, actually the most important of all productive factors, we would die without it. However, this productive factor is not scarce and therefore nobody ever came up with the idea that it must be paid for.

As far as land is concerned the classic idea that it is scarce has been qualified over the last 200 years. We can neglect that.

Many people assume that capital, i.e. money, is a scarce productive factor. They assume that something that is scarce for themselves must be scarce in general. Central banks have proved over the last 10 years, we are still in 2015, that it can be printed in any amount.

In Keynesian theory there is only one productive factor left which actually has a price and therefore must be remunerated: labour.

[This should not be confused with Marxist nonsense. It is true that both in classical theory and in Marxism only work creates value, but the argument is completely different. In classical theory and in Marxism labour produces capital, but in Keynesianism there is, except in a situation of full employment, no need for capital in the sense of a productive factor. In Keynesian theory it has no price, which will lead in the long run to the death of the functionless rentier.]

The Marxist capitalist will not be expropriated by the proletarians of the world, but by the central banks, if the proletarians of the world have the same know-how as the capitalists. Know-how actually is a productive factor. The most important one of all of them.

Due to the fact that Keynesian theory is not understood, we can read and hear on a daily basis that Keynes is kind of a "socialist", although the basic principles of a market economy, competition and decentralised information processing through prices, remain completely untouched by Keynesian theory.

Lowering the interest rate has no impact on the allocation of productive resources, because money isn't, in case of unemployment, a productive resource and fiscal policy only activates idle resources and therefore misallocation is difficult to achieve, because idle resources have already reached the maximum of misallocation. They just do not produce anything.

The only productive resource which actually must be remunerated is labour, especially qualified labour. This kind of labour is scarce and the price for labour, the wage, is a price in the sense of the market economy. Without wages signaling scarcity there is no need in the labour market for an adaptation to structural changes.

What has to be said concerning expansive fiscal policy has already be said in chapter III.2.

Let's remember the title of the book. The book is called "General Theory of Employment, Interest and Money". It would be a step in the right direction if people were to remember the title of the book in public debate and in textbooks about macroeconomics.

A general theory of employment, interest and money is not a cyclical theory, as we can hear and read everywhere. It is a fundamental discussion about employment, interest and money, regardless of the different phases of the cycle. Money is never the same thing as capital. Not in economic downturn, not in recession, not in depression, not in recovery and not in boom times. Never. The interest rate is never the price for money in the sense of a market economy. Never.

The labour market depends on the market for goods and the market for goods depends on the money market. This is true for downturn, recession, recovery and boom.

We can read as well that Keynes didn't understand the difference between classical theory and neoclassical theory. This is nonsense. He understood the difference perfectly well, but as far as employment, money and interest rates are concerned there is no difference between classical and neoclassical theory, and therefore a distinction is not needed, and Keynes didn't distinguish.

Keynesianism it not about expansive fiscal policy and it is still less about anti-cyclical intervention. That is a possible conclusion that can be drawn from Keynesian theory, but not its main message. If the problem were only economic cycles, the problem wouldn't be very serious and there would be little need for intervention. The problem would be resolved automatically. Keynesian theory suggests the opposite. Recession and depression can be lasting phenomena.

The most difficult part of the title is "General Theory". Why does the title say "General Theory"?

Classical economics assumes full employment.

(Actually there is a small difference between authors like David Ricardo (classical) and Léon Walras (neoclassical). In the theory of David Ricardo capital is needed to employ workers. If there is only a little disposable capital, fewer people are employed. Wages always remain at subsistence level. In the work of Léon Walras wages correspond to marginal revenue and capital is competing with labour. In both cases capital is a productive factor, which it is not in Keynesian theory.)

Full employment is only a special case, and Keynesian theory is compatible with both cases, unemployment and with full employment.

In the case of full employment we have a situation comparable to the microeconomics perspective and there is no need to distinguish between capital and money. At a microeconomic level capital and money for investment purposes are the result of not-consumed income of the past and sacrifice was needed to obtain it. At a microeconomic level money is scarce and scarce things have a price.

In a situation of full employment, and this distinction doesn't even exist in classical thinking, it is necessary save money, because saving means less consumption and in a situation of full employment, the production of capital goods, which is necessary for a higher production of consumer goods in the future, is only possible if the production of consumer goods is reduced in the present and the productive resources are reallocated.

In this situation the price for money or capital is a price in a market sense. The higher the price for money, i.e. the interest rate, the more people will save money and reduce their consumption.

For this special case, full employment, we arrive at the same results if we assume Keynesian monetary mechanisms. If national income is high, the need for money for transaction purposes is high as well, and we approach full employment. In this situation there is no speculative fund left and any further increase of national income can only be achieved by selling securities. That leads to a lower price for securities, and thus to a higher return on securities. This will lead to an increase in savings, which is necessary in this situation. The argument is completely different than in classical theory, but the result is the same. Any increase in the money supply would lead, if accepted by the market, to inflation.

(That's by the way the constellation assumed by monetarism. Higher inflation would lead to a higher demand for money for transaction purposes, which can only be satisfied by selling securities. Their prices will fall and so will the return, and therefore the interest rate will increase. The fact that monetarism is considered a new economic theory is due to the fact that Keynesian theory is not understood. The general theory includes monetarism as well. For a more detailed discussion the reader is referred to the www. economics-reloaded.com.)

In the case of full employment classical theory and Keynesianism arrive at the same results. The price for money has an allocation function in the sense of a market economy. The scarcity of money guarantees that consumption is reduced in favour of investment, because the first is not profitable at all.

In the case of unemployment, a situation simply inexistent in classical theory, the situation is different. Classical theory and Keynesian theory arrive at completely different results. Classical theory assumes that capital is scarce. In order to employ more people, capital is needed. The problem can only be overcome by higher interest rates, which leads to more savings and more disposable capital for investment purposes.

In Keynesian theory the interest rate, determined far away from the markets for goods on the money market, is the hurdle which impedes further investments.

In other words: Classical theory says that in a situation of unemployment high interest rates induce people to invest more and therefore provide the capital necessary to create jobs. In Keynesian theory high interest rates are a hurdle for investments. The difference is that capital in classical theory is a productive factor that can only be obtained by sacrificing present consumption for future consumption. In Keynesian theory capital, i.e. money, is no productive factor, it can be obtained without any sacrifice, and it is not even possible to transfer present consumption to future consumption by saving.

From the title "General Theory..." we can deduce as well that the book is a theory about the causal relationships between economic variables. But public debate doesn't focus on the theory, but on the conclusions that can eventually be drawn from this theory and depending on their underlying political conviction people see Keynesian theory refuted or confirmed. If you want to refute Keynesian theory you must address the theoretical concepts and not the conclusions some people draw from this theory.

Actually there is no public discussion about Keynesian theory. The book is a general theory about employment, interest and money. Keynes refutes the concepts of the classics about employment, interest and money. But there is no discussion about interest and money. Public debate not only refuses to take into account the content of the book, actually nobody has read it. Public debate doesn't even care about the title of the book, although the title is very precise in this case and obviously the result of reflection. There is no other book about economics with such a consciously chosen title.

Last but not least the book is about employment. Classical economics assumes that in the long run an equilibrium is always reached on the three markets, the labour market, the goods market and the capital market, the latter substituted by Keynes by the money market.

Keynes's argument is sophisticated, but it can be simplified. Interest rates are fixed on the money market, and it would be a mere coincidence if these interest rates lead to full employment.

In classical theory interest rates equal savings and investment. High interest rates will lead to an increase of savings and to a decrease of investment, in the opposite case it will be the other way round. Finally we will reach an equilibrium, where neither the investors nor the savers will change their decisions.

Due to the fact that the only alternative to consumption is saving and investing, all the supply will be absorbed by demand. In this sense the interest rate is a price in the sense of a market economy.

If we take into account that what the savers save is actually money, and not capital, and that the investors need capital in its most liquid form, namely money, we will arrive at a different conclusion. The interest rate is determined on the money market, something inexistent in classical economics. None of the assumptions of classical theory is valid anymore, as pointed out in III.1.

It could be argued in a more simple way. The interest rate is simply fixed by the central banks. However, this is as irrelevant for Keynesian theory as the fact that Keynes abstracts completely from the organisation of the money market and its institutional implementation.

The crucial point is that the goods markets compete with the money market, and the money market is in the stronger position. If global GPD is $70 trillion and the turnover on the stock markets alone is $30 trillion we can easily imagine what would happen if all this money would be used in a productive way.

In classical theory money is just a veil. If the amount of money doubles, the prices double as well, but the relationship between the prices remains unchanged.

In Keynsian theory money plays a crucial role, because money is needed to invest, not capital in the sense of non-consumed income of the past. It is irrelevant where this money comes from, if it derives from non-consumed income of the past, or if it is just printed by the central banks, but one must have it.

This money has an ambivalent character. On the one hand it is not scarce, and on the other it determines the interest rate real investments have to compete with.

To put it simple: In classical theory people would consume their money if a real investment seems too risky. In this case money would induce a demand. Unfortunately they have an alternative, and that's the crucial point of Keynesian theory: They can invest in something almost as liquid as money, in listed securities.

These points of Keynesian theory have not been refuted, they have not even been discussed. Actually there is no discussion about Keynesian theory. There is only a discussion about some conclusions that can be drawn from Keynesian theory. Keynesian theory is difficult to understand for most people, because it contradicts their personal experience. From an individual point of view money and capital is the same thing, it is scarce, it has a price, it is a production factor and sacrifice is needed to obtain it and they will invest it in the most profitable way. Individuals can't produce money out of nothing.

At a macroeconomic level all that is not true. Money is not scarce, therefore it doesn't have a price, it has no impact on allocation. In a situation of underemployment there is no need to stop less profitable investments in favour of more profitable ones.

At an individual level it is crystal-clear that money must be put to the most profitable use. But it is crystal-clear as well that at a macroeconomic level, when there are enough resources to realise the profitable and the less profitable investments, both should be realised.

If we think about it a little bit, we quickly realise that even common sense can understand that something valid at a microeconomic level is not true at a macroeconomic level.

We can hear and read as well that some people want a microeconomic foundation of Keynesian theory. Something like that doesn't exist. The message of Keynes is clear: Rational behaviour at the microeconomic level can be very irrational at the macroeconomic level.

A meaningful debate about macroeconomic issues is not possible without Keynesian theory.

The public and academic economists are completely unaware of the scope of Keynesian theory, although everybody knows the name. Every night the public channels treat us to explanations about stock prices. They are paid for explaining what is going on and not for obscuring reality with confusing explanations.

Quoted shares are nothing but a beauty contest, there is no rationality behind them. The players on this market, the stock market, don't do anything but constantly trying to second-guess each other. Listed shares are the presumptions about the presumption of other people.

Shares are praised as a good investment because in the long run their price will always rise. It is to assume that reality is more complicated. The stock market is a redistribution machine and on average the small investors will lose money, because they are not able to manipulate the prices and are less well informed. A surplus that can be distributed and not redistributed derives only from the dividends, but these have become more and more irrelevant. The real business is speculating on the rise and fall of stock prices.

More interesting than the question whether stock prices rise or fall is the question who lost and who earned money, and we know very little about this really interesting issue.

Besides the increase in assets in this case only exists on paper. If the increased assets are consumed, actually their only useful use, this demand must be satisfied and that happens in the real economy or it doesn't happen.

The conclusions to be drawn from Keynesian theory are therefore very simple. An increase in wealth can only be obtained through knowledge, because knowledge is the only productive factor – and that was stated long before Keynes, by Alfred Marshall.

www.ingramcontent.com/pod-product-compliance
Lightning Source LLC
Chambersburg PA
CBHW080619180526
45168CB00007B/2978